AF484640

Whispers of Romance

Sunaina Aggarwal

INDIA · SINGAPORE · MALAYSIA

Copyright © Sunaina Aggrawal 2025
All Rights Reserved.

ISBN 979-8-89699-969-0

This book has been published with all efforts taken to make the material error-free after the consent of the author. However, the author and the publisher do not assume and hereby disclaim any liability to any party for any loss, damage, or disruption caused by errors or omissions, whether such errors or omissions result from negligence, accident, or any other cause.

While every effort has been made to avoid any mistake or omission, this publication is being sold on the condition and understanding that neither the author nor the publishers or printers would be liable in any manner to any person by reason of any mistake or omission in this publication or for any action taken or omitted to be taken or advice rendered or accepted on the basis of this work. For any defect in printing or binding the publishers will be liable only to replace the defective copy by another copy of this work then available.

Disclaimer

The illustrations in this book have been inspired by various doodles available on Pinterest and other sources. Some have been modified or adapted for artistic purposes. If any original artist feels their work has been used without proper acknowledgment, we are open to making necessary adjustments.

Whispers of Romance

Table of contents

" Tweets "

"*Just the two of us, sharing one cup of coffee or tea whatever you like, as the rain beautifully dances around us.*"

" If you get the moon by mistake, the moon will no longer be the moon as you would never value it, some things are meant to be cherised only as desire."

" You are my love and my conflict, the start of my story and the conclusion of my souls journey, everything I am in every way, starts and ends with you."

" *A woman's shyness is a reflection of her deep connectiom to the man who holds her heart, revealing the depth of her affection and vulnerability.*"

" It is a longing meant to remain a longing, if it were to become reality, the depth of love it holds might become too heavy and profound for my heart to endure, knowing it can never be truly mine."

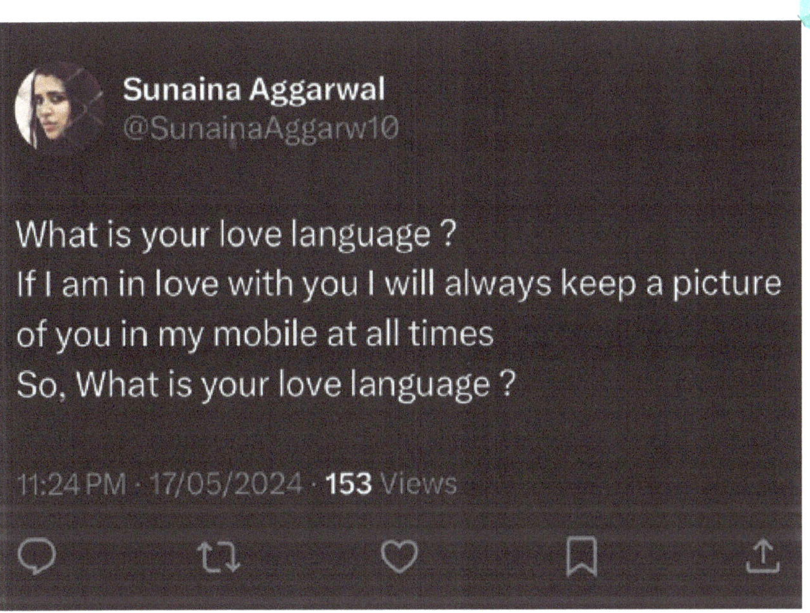

" *So, what is your love language that transcends words,
speaking instead through the actions that reveal your
true feelings ?* "

"So, who is your bonfire ?,the one who ignites your warmth and lights up your soul. "

"So, who is that one person you wish upon fallen stars with,hoping to share a timeless connection ? "

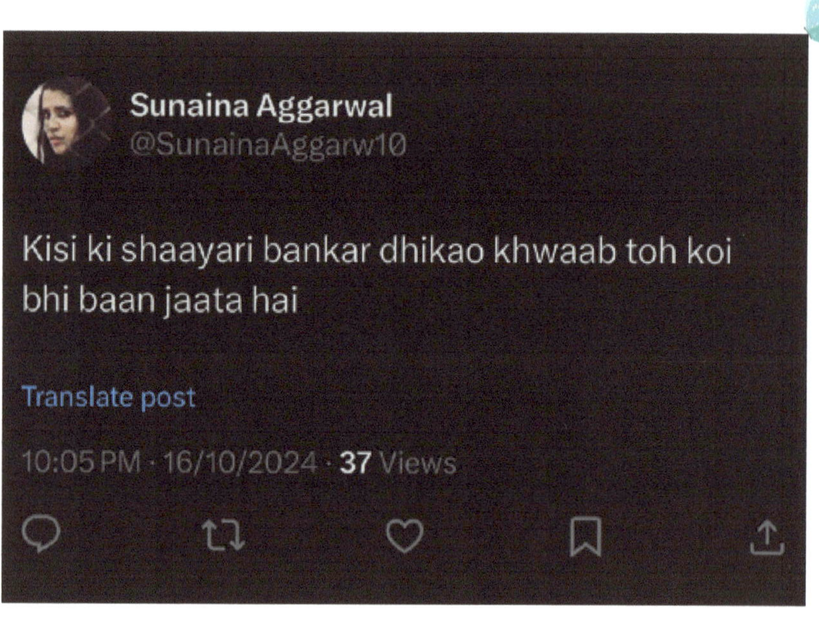

"Be somone's poetry, as anyone can become a dream."

Chats

Jaana zaruri hai ?

" *I must go, though my heart remains with you,*
for every moment apart will only bring
me closer to you , as if my soul is destined
to return to yours, for no distance can change
the truth that we are two halves of a
single soul forever drawn back to
each other."

Aapse gussa ho jaayu
toh ?

"And if I grow angry with you ?
I'll speak to your picture, for it if it's
not you, then there's only emptiness
only you, now and forever no one else."

Diwali aa rahi hai

mere ghar ki Lakshmi
banke aana

" Diwali is nearing, come into my life,
the Goddess Lakshmi of my life."

Kya chhate ho ?

Tumhe chhata hoon

" What do you desire ?
It's you whom I desire."

Sabse pyaari cheez

Uski saadgi

*" The most precious beauty of all
is the quiet elegance of her simplicity."*

Kya khwahish hai ?

" *What is your only wish ?*
To belong to her, and take those
seven vows with her, wrapped in the warmth
of the sacred fire."

Sabse sundar ?

Uski yeh ankhein

" Admist all the world's beauty,
it's her eyes that hold the deepest magic."

Kaal Karwachauth hai

*" Tomorrow is Karva Chauth,
but you are the only moon my heart
seeks and yearns for."*

Dimaag mein kya chal raha hai ?

"What thoughts fill your mind ?"
"Only you."

What is your life without me ?

I wish I was blind if I can't
see your presence

"*What is life without you ?*
I would choose darkness over sight if
it meant i could no longer feel the
warmth and heartbeat of your
presence beside me."

Thankyou for reading

You + me = 💕

www.ingramcontent.com/pod-product-compliance
Lightning Source LLC
Chambersburg PA
CBHW040919110726
48005CB00006B/951